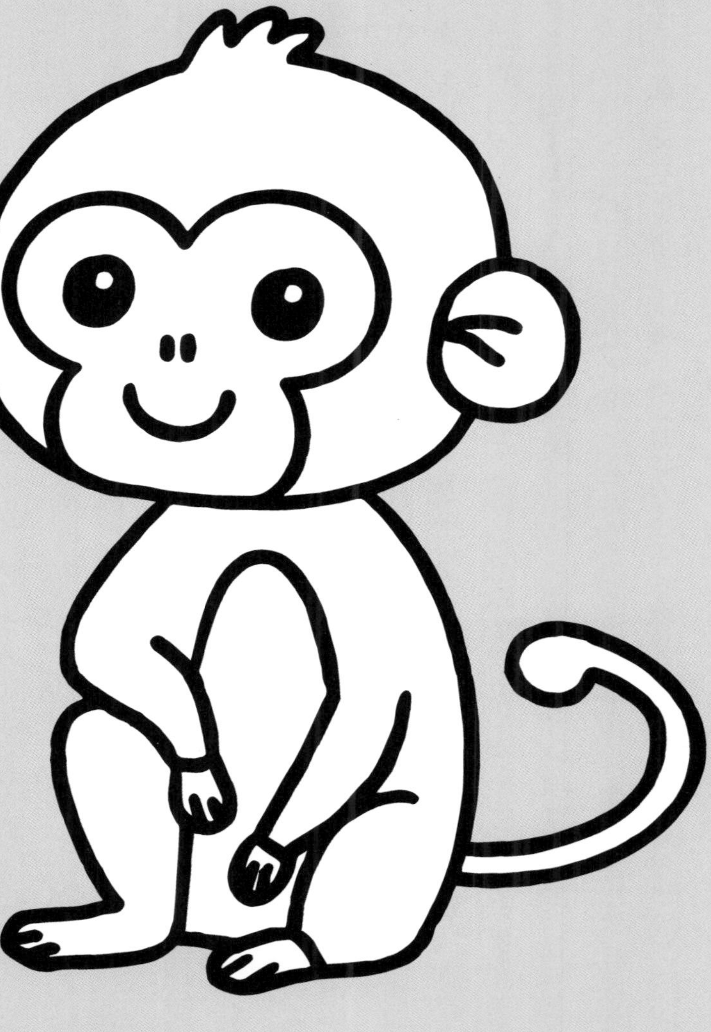

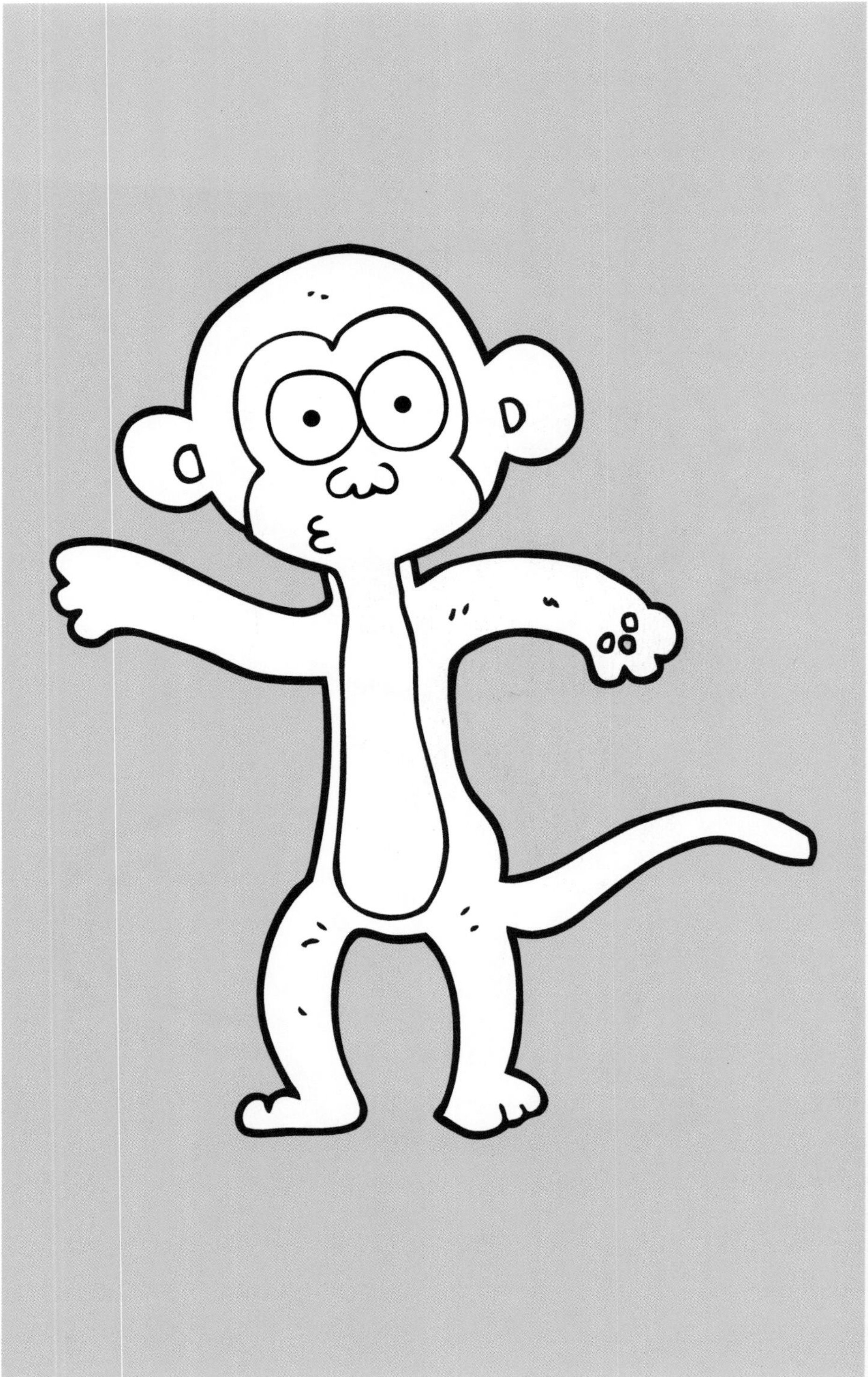

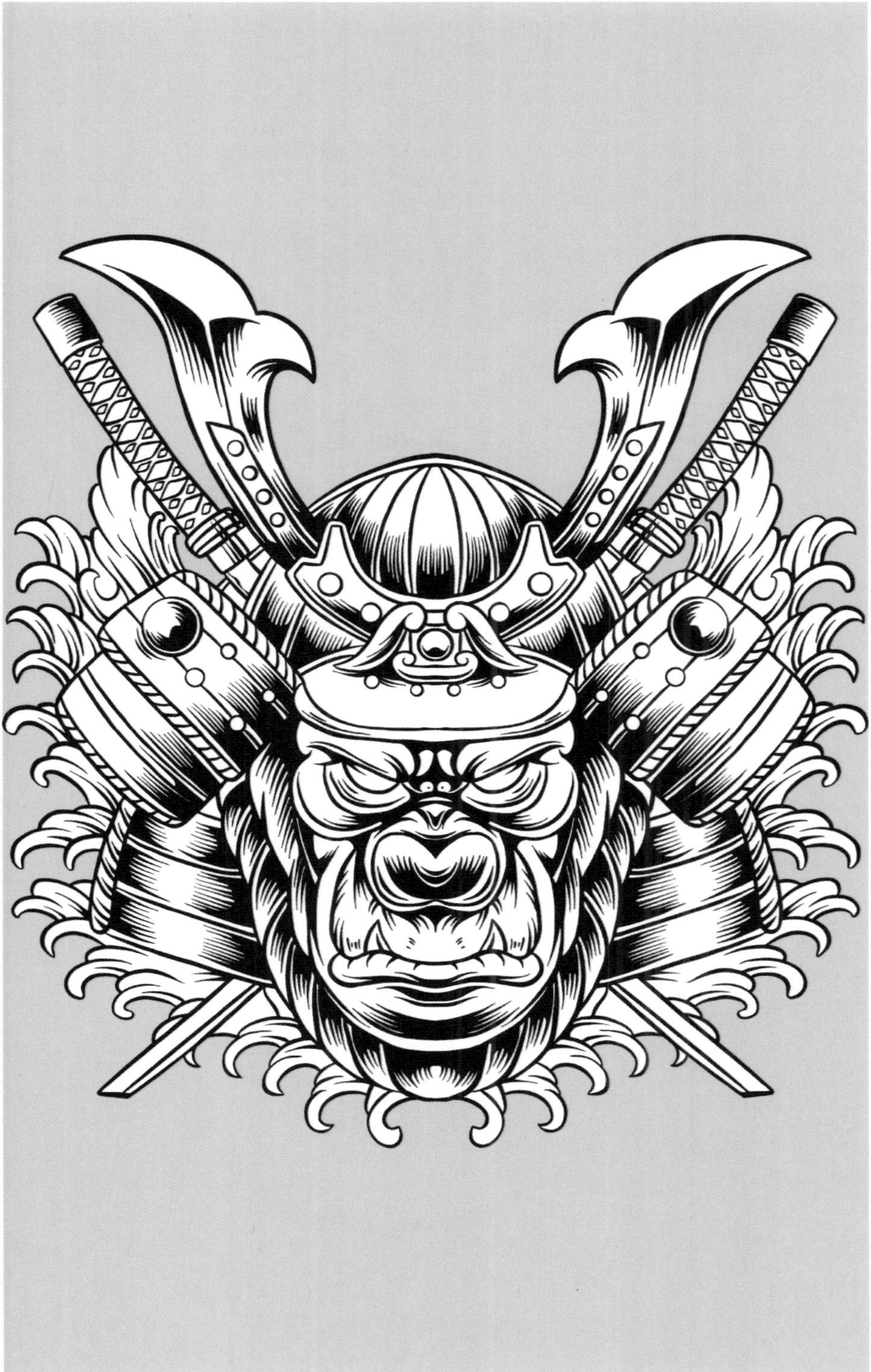

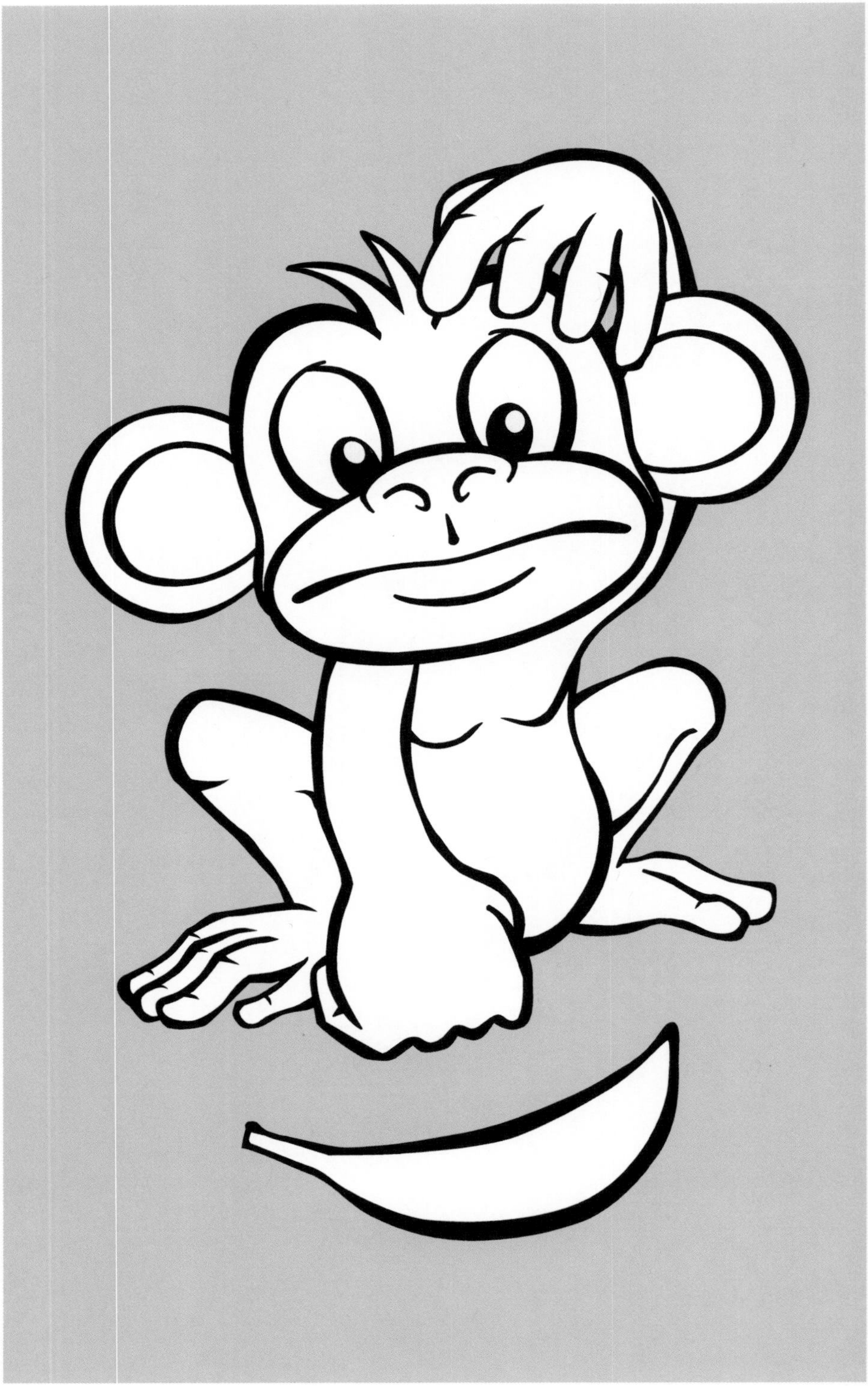

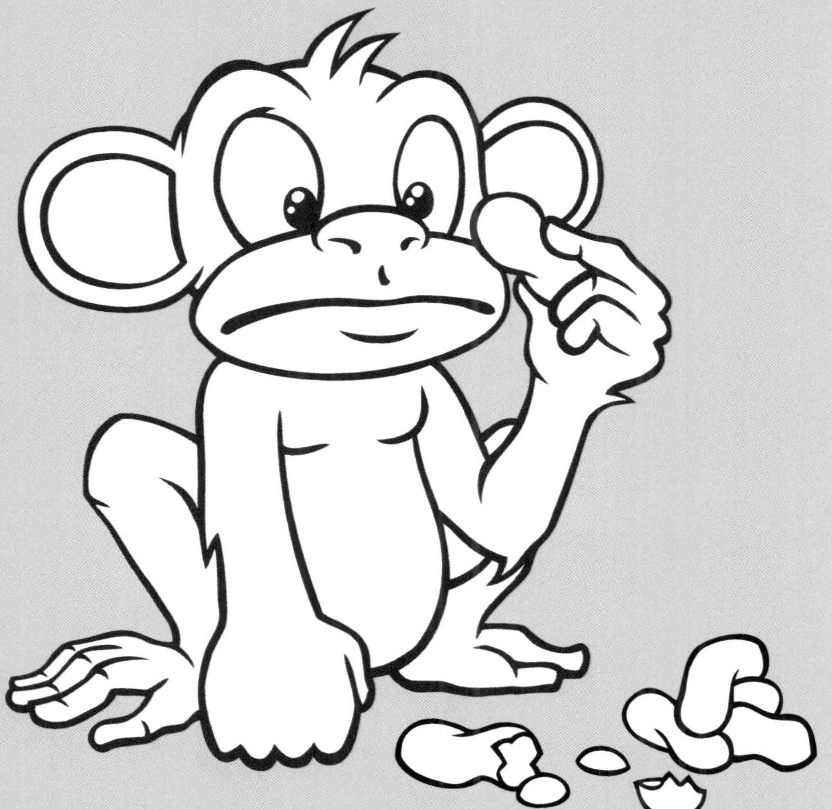

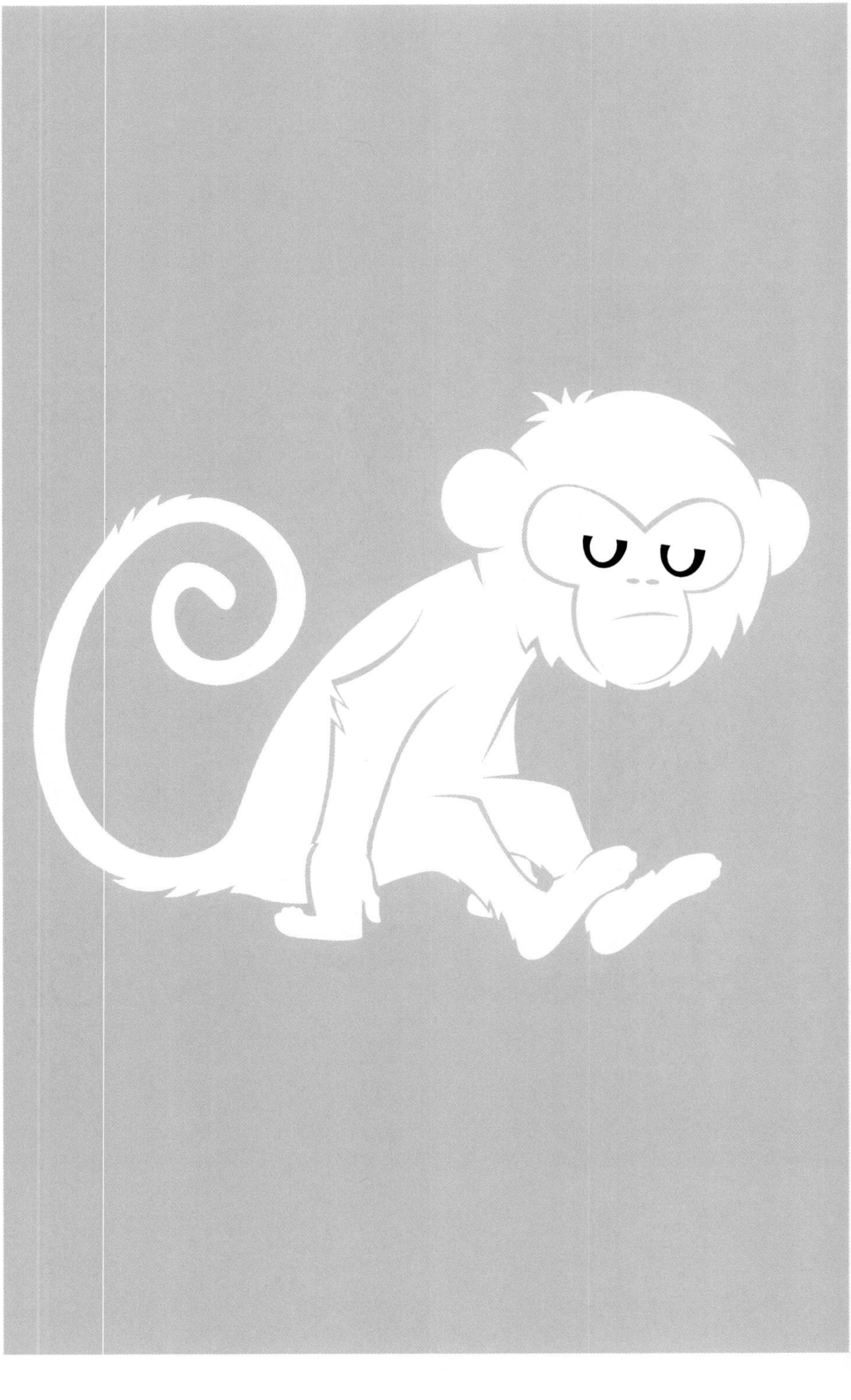

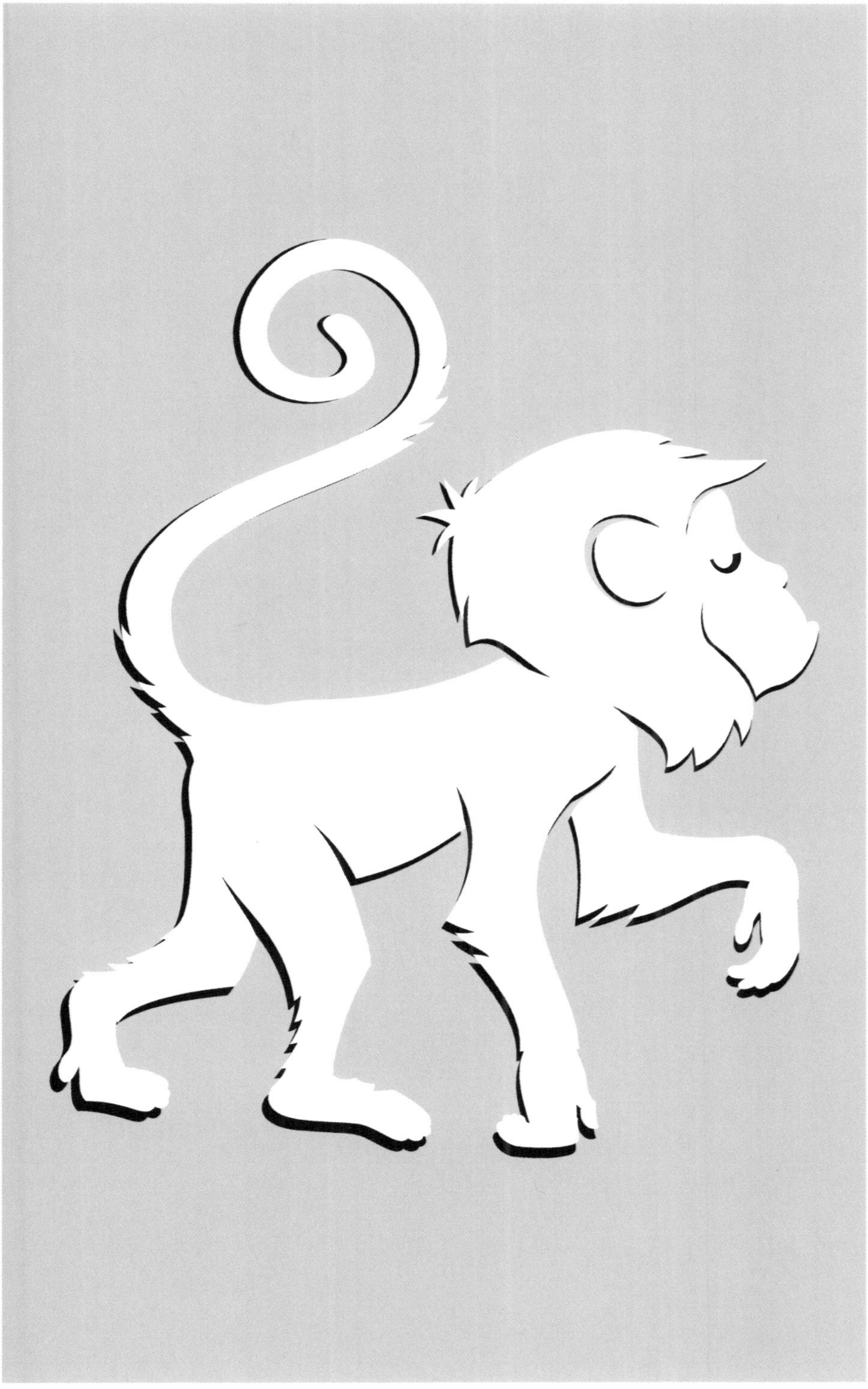

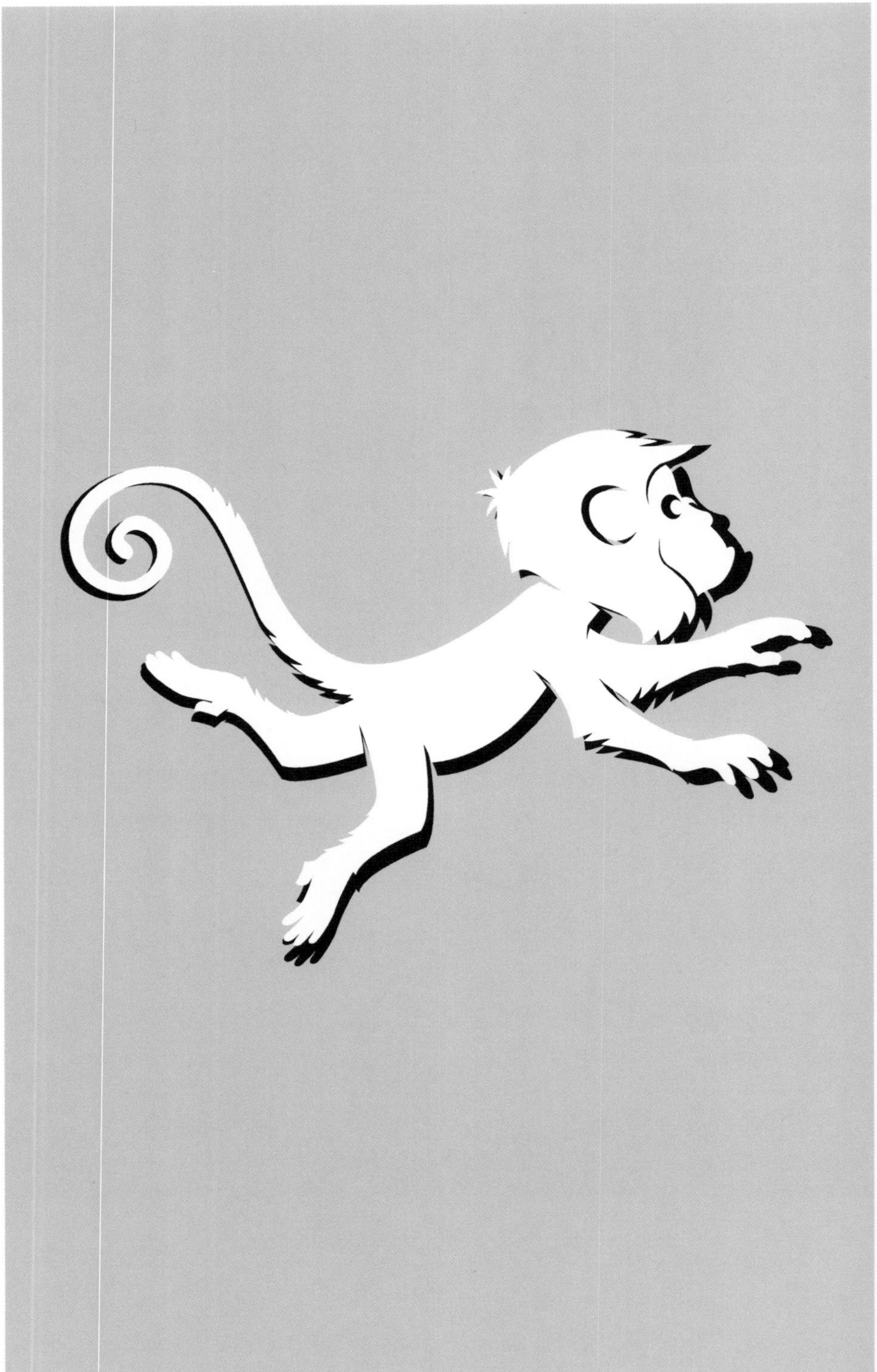

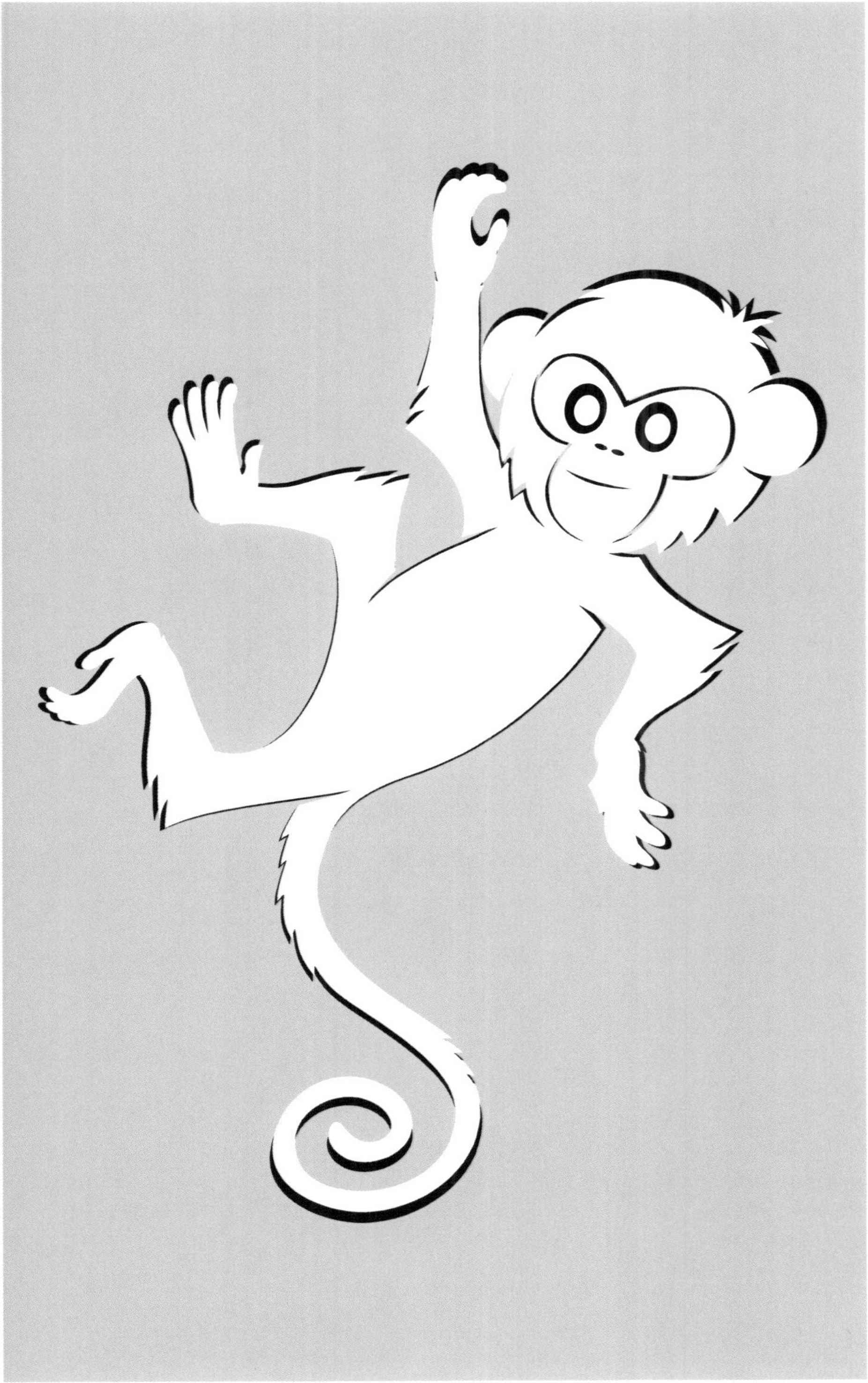

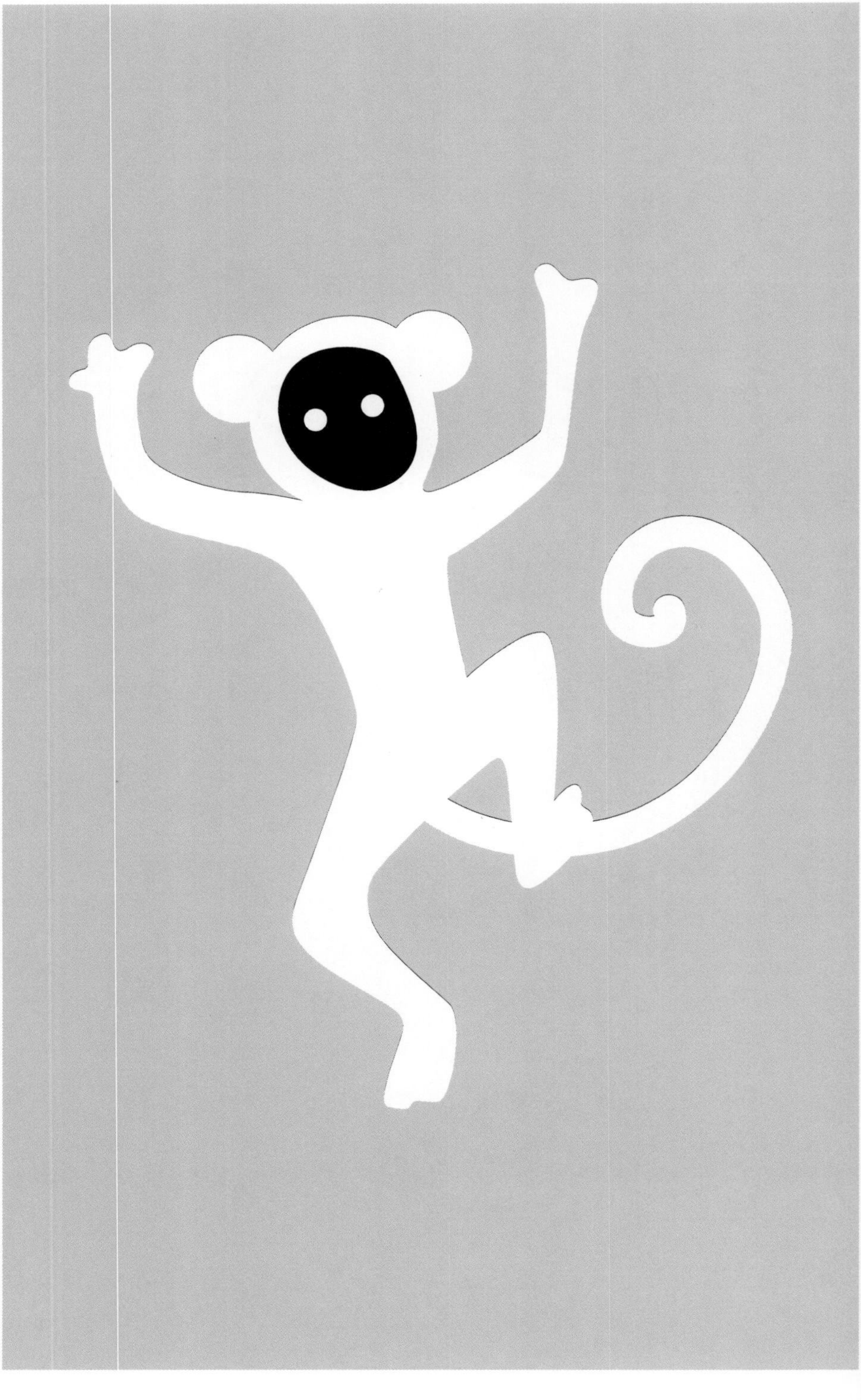

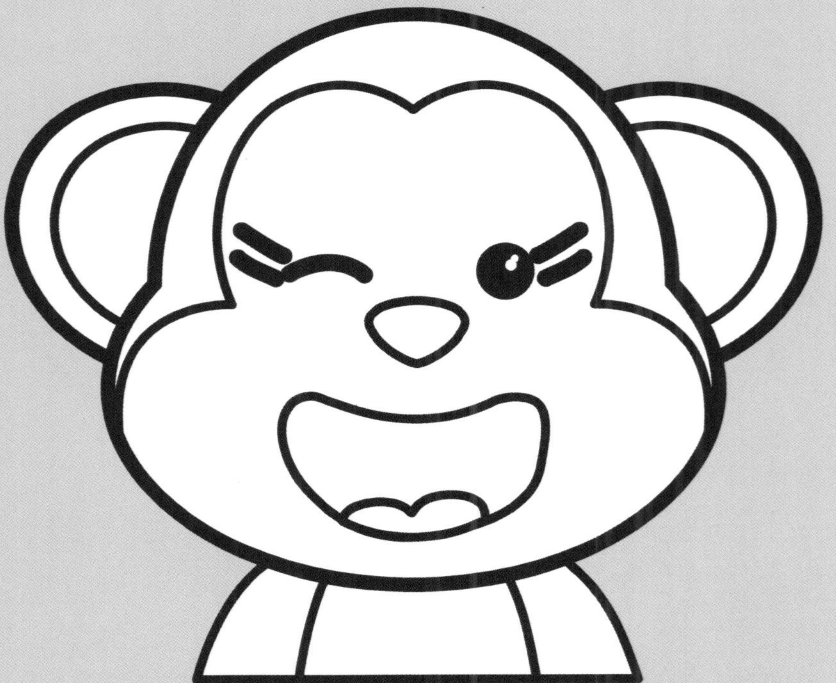

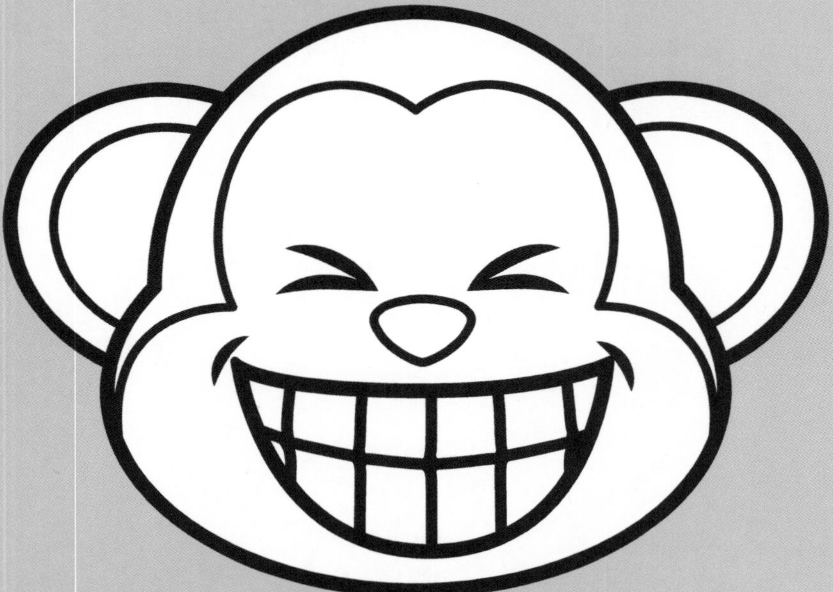

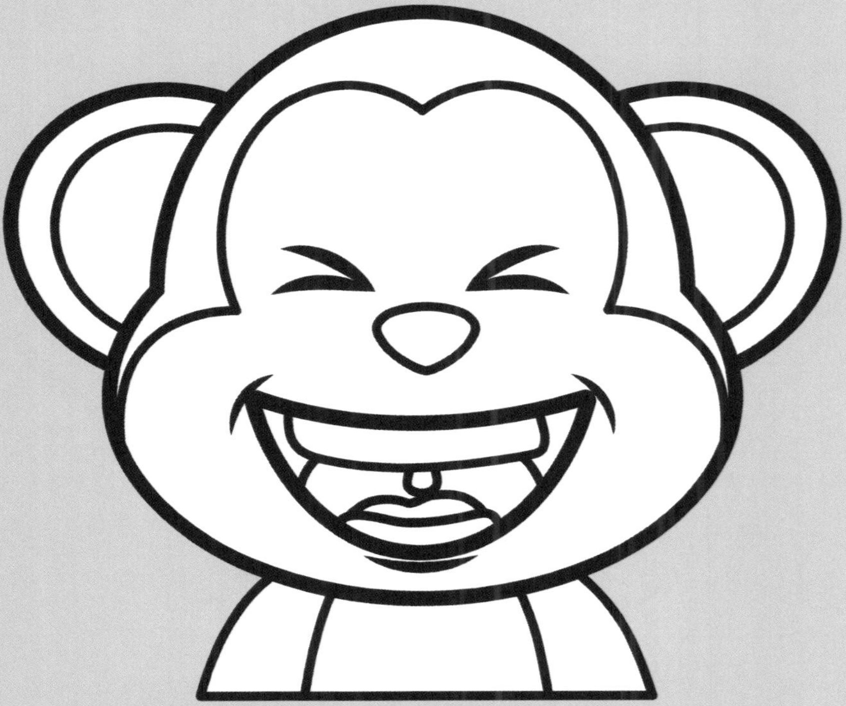

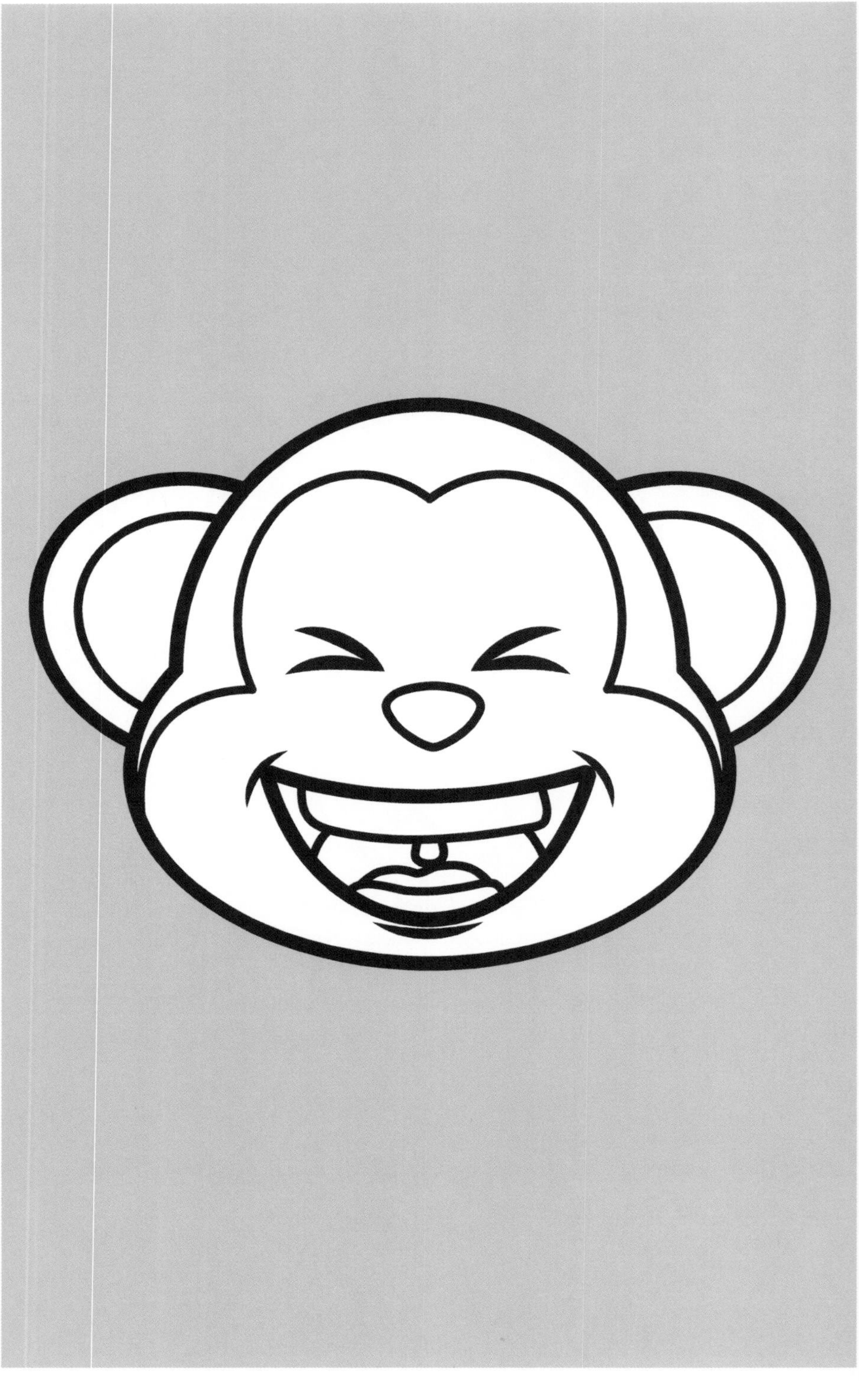

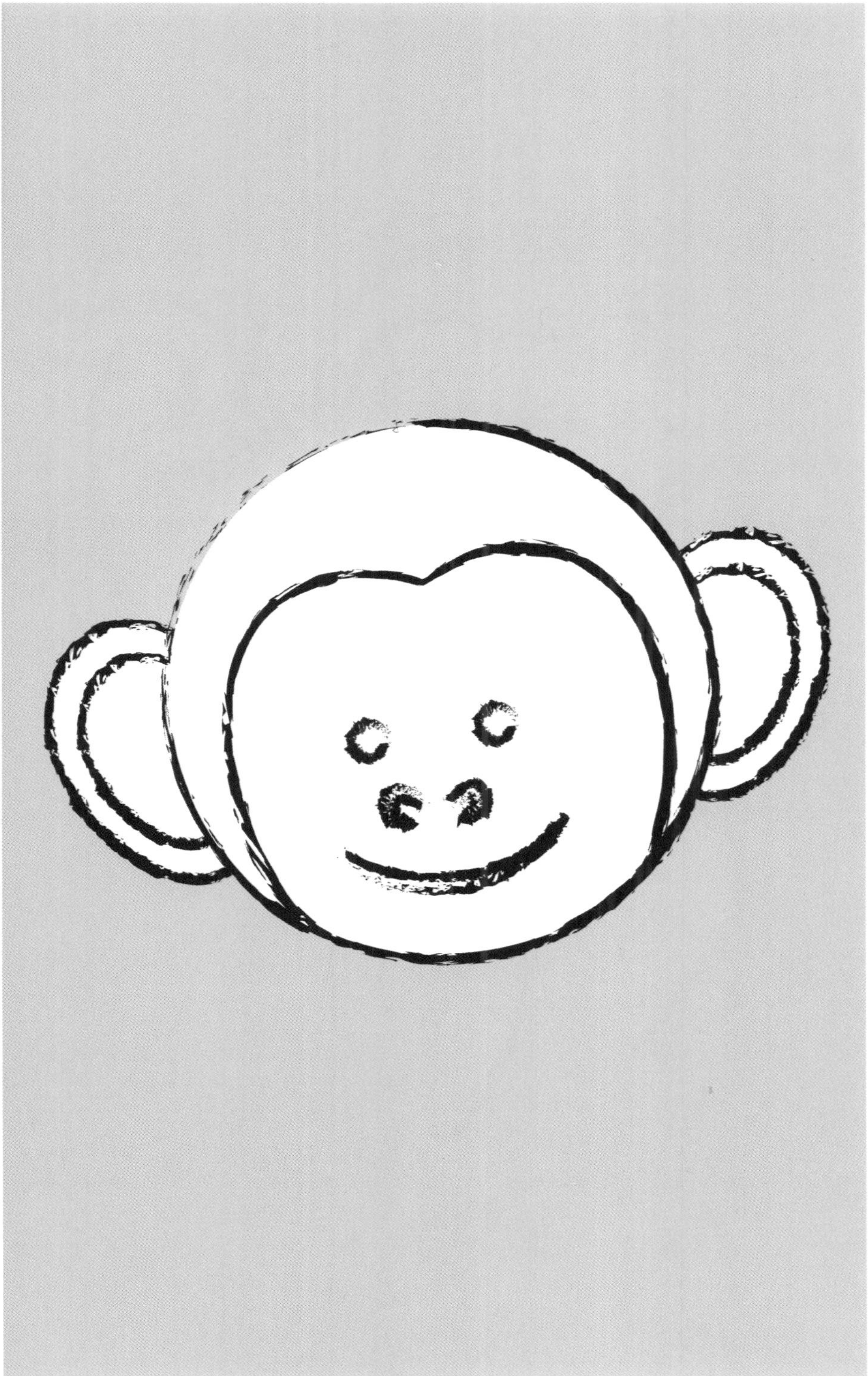

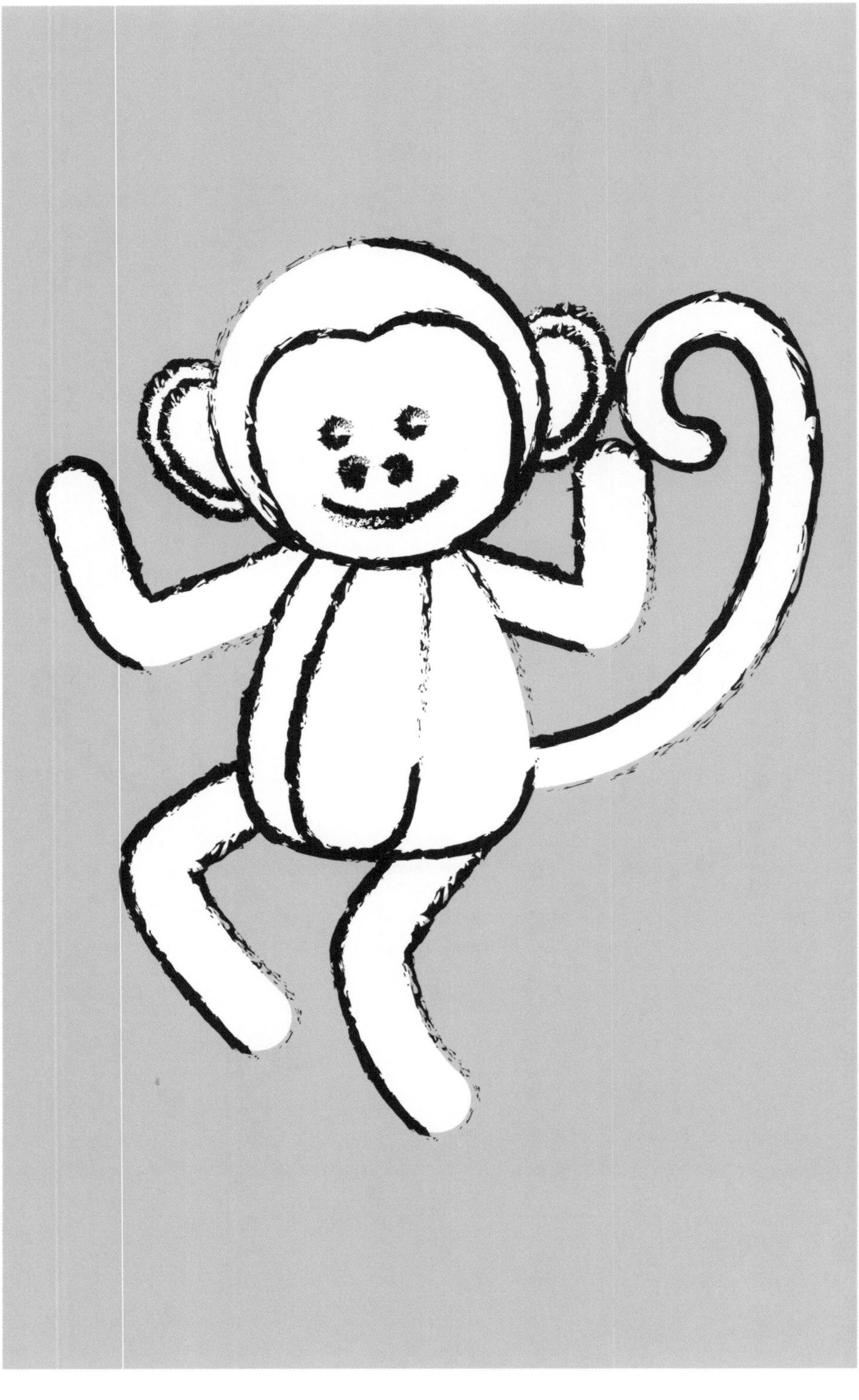

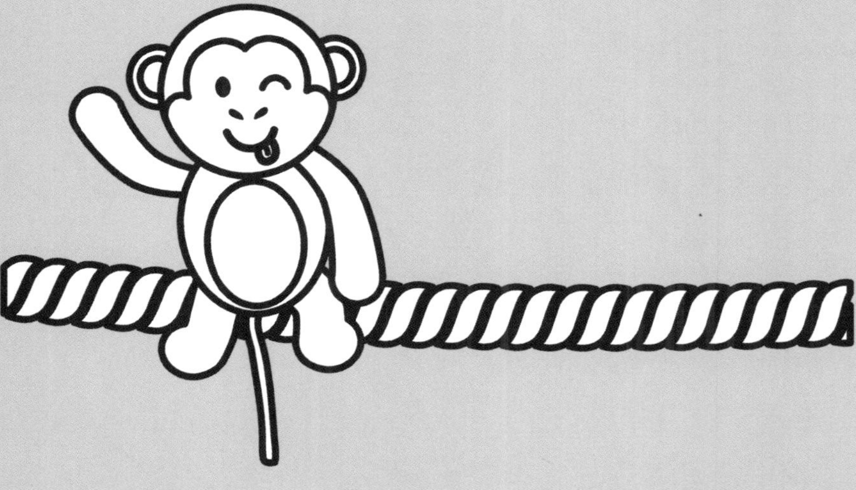

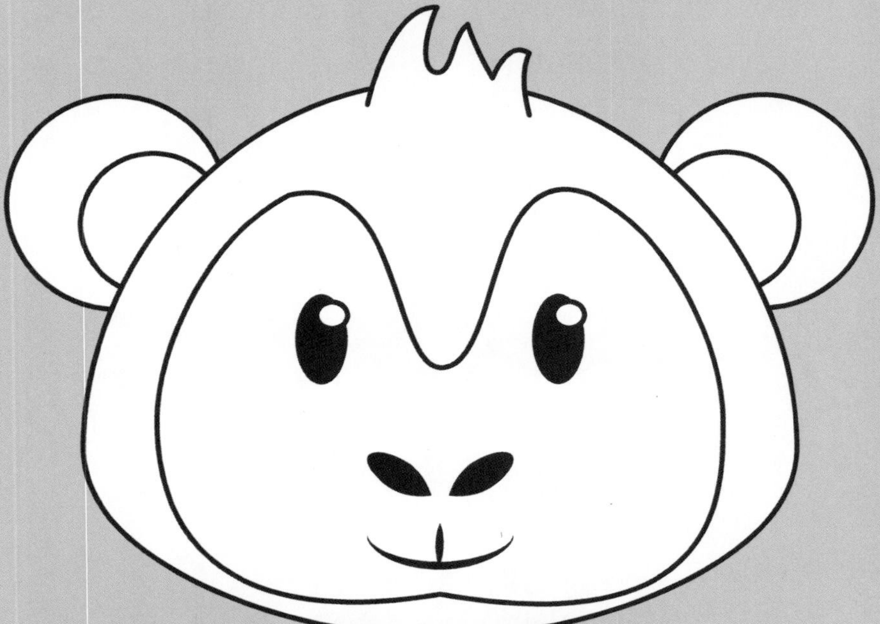

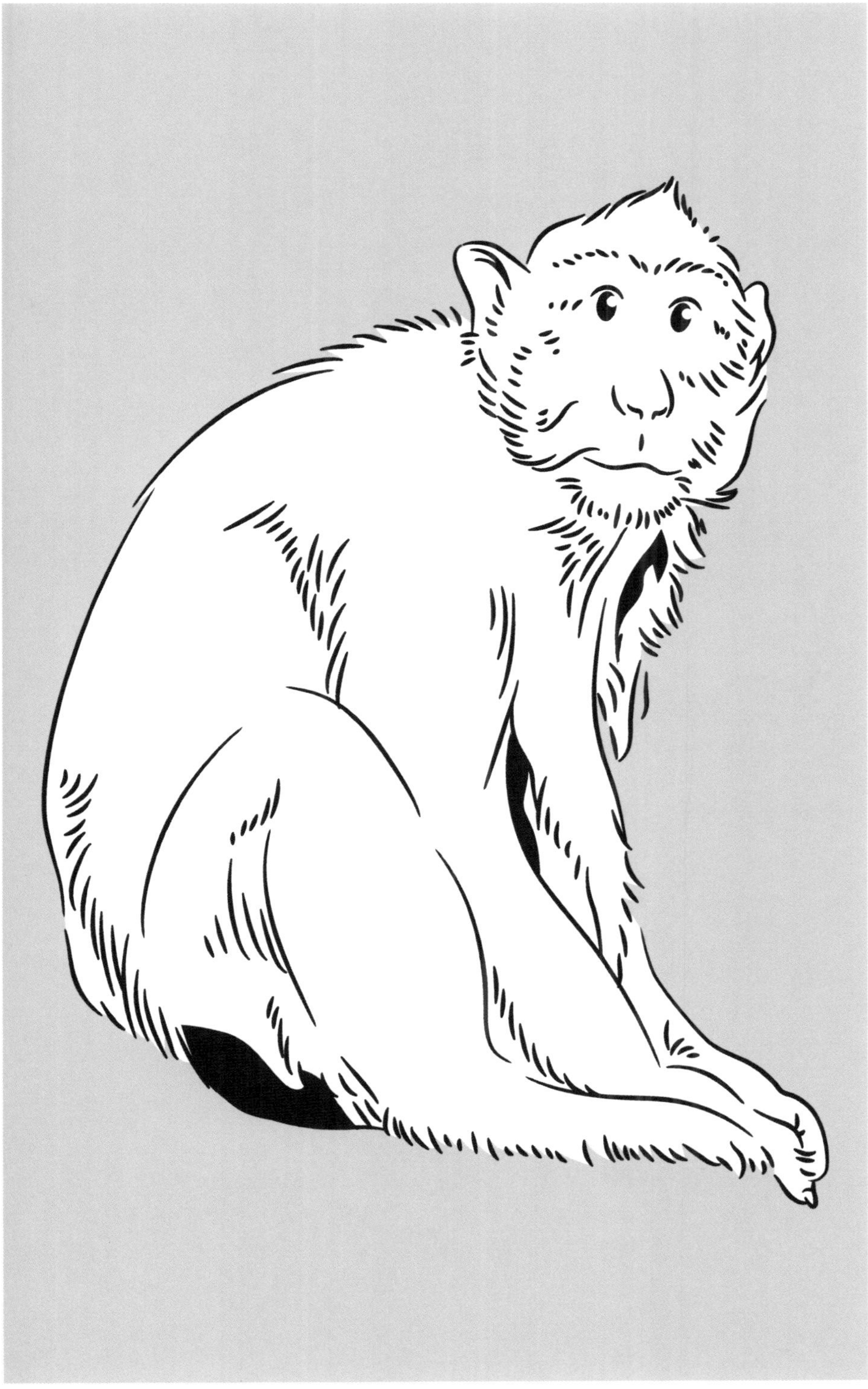

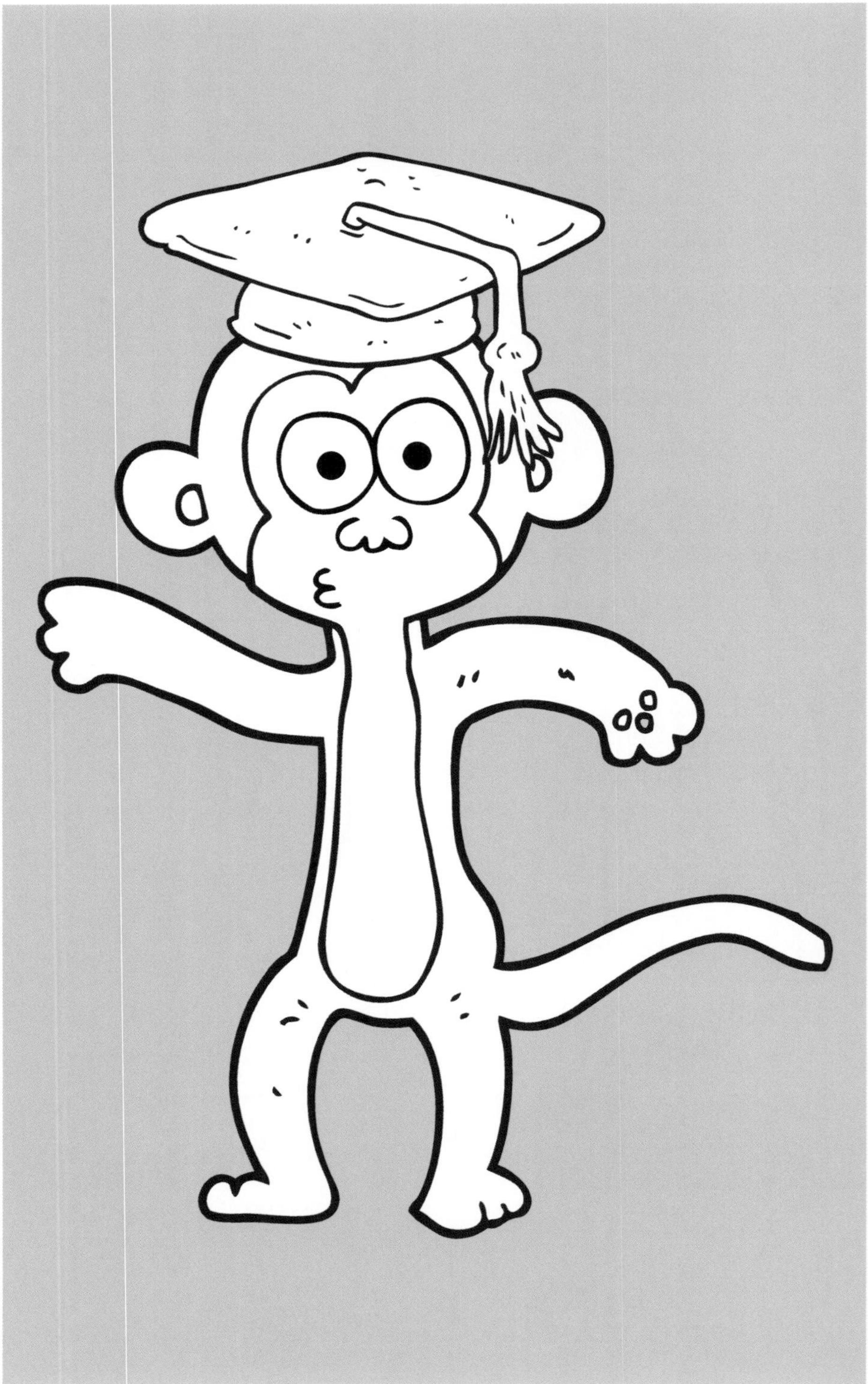

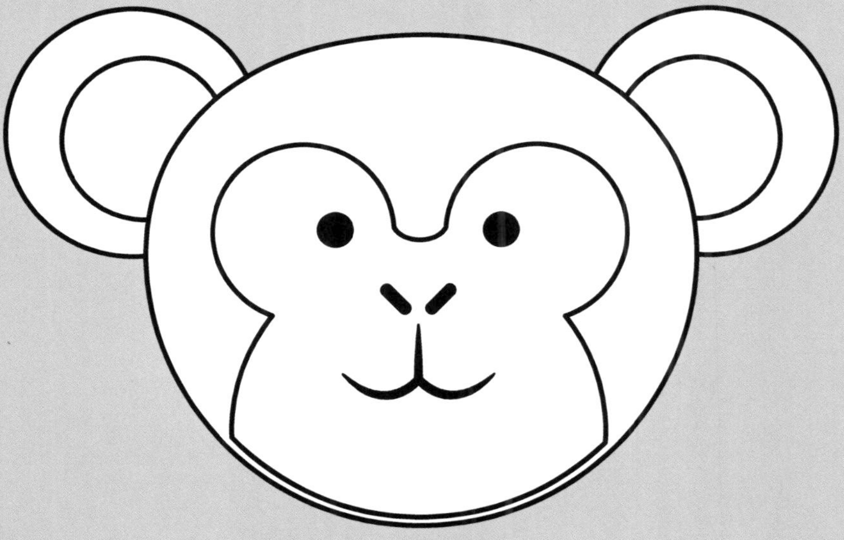

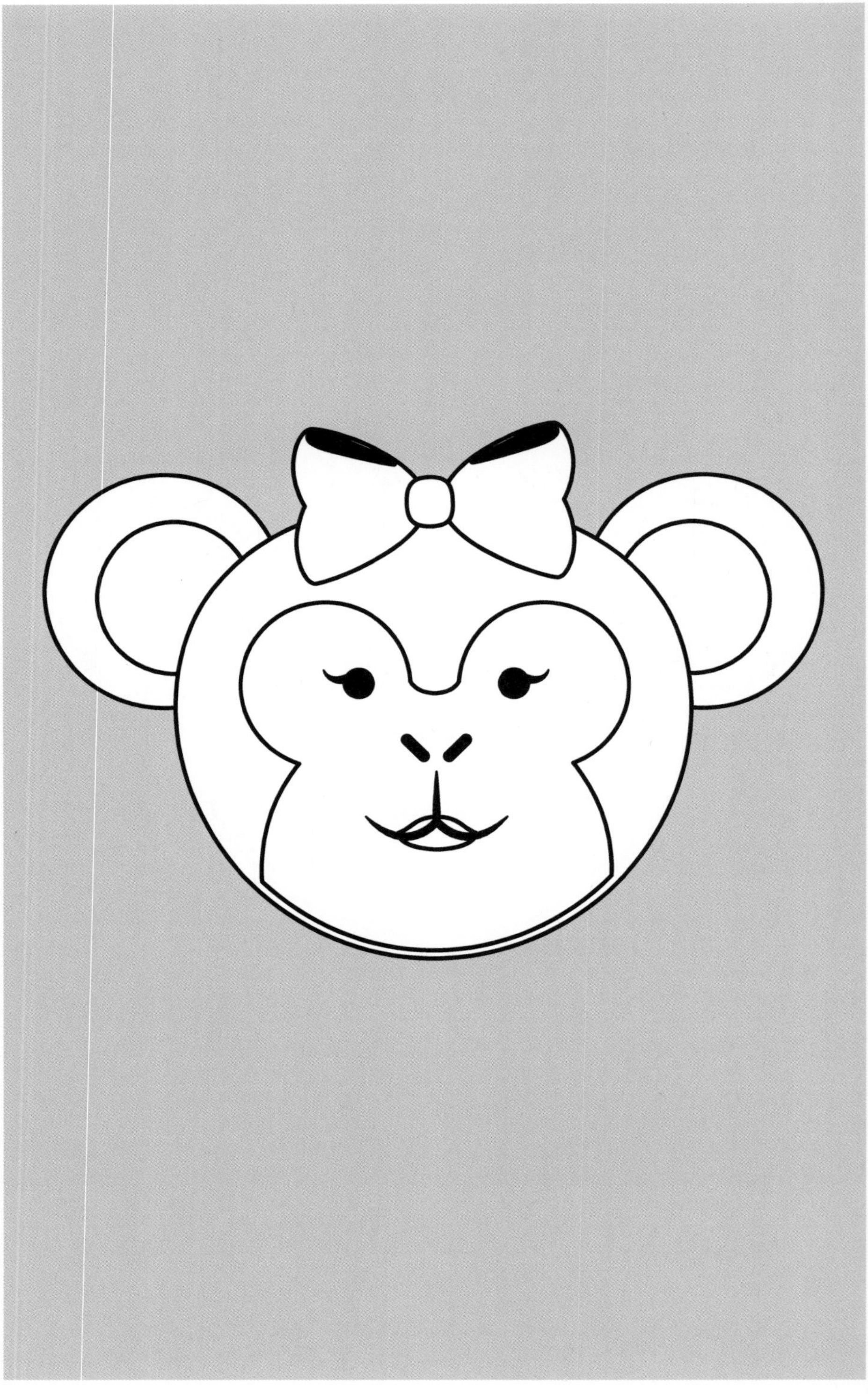

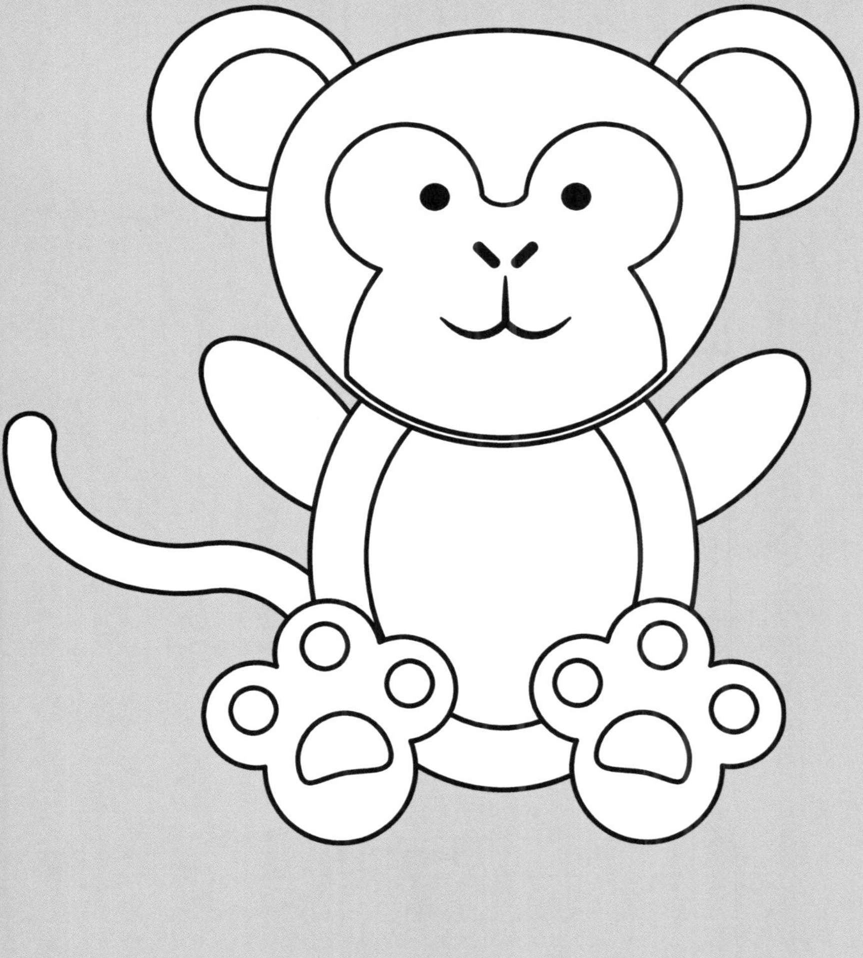

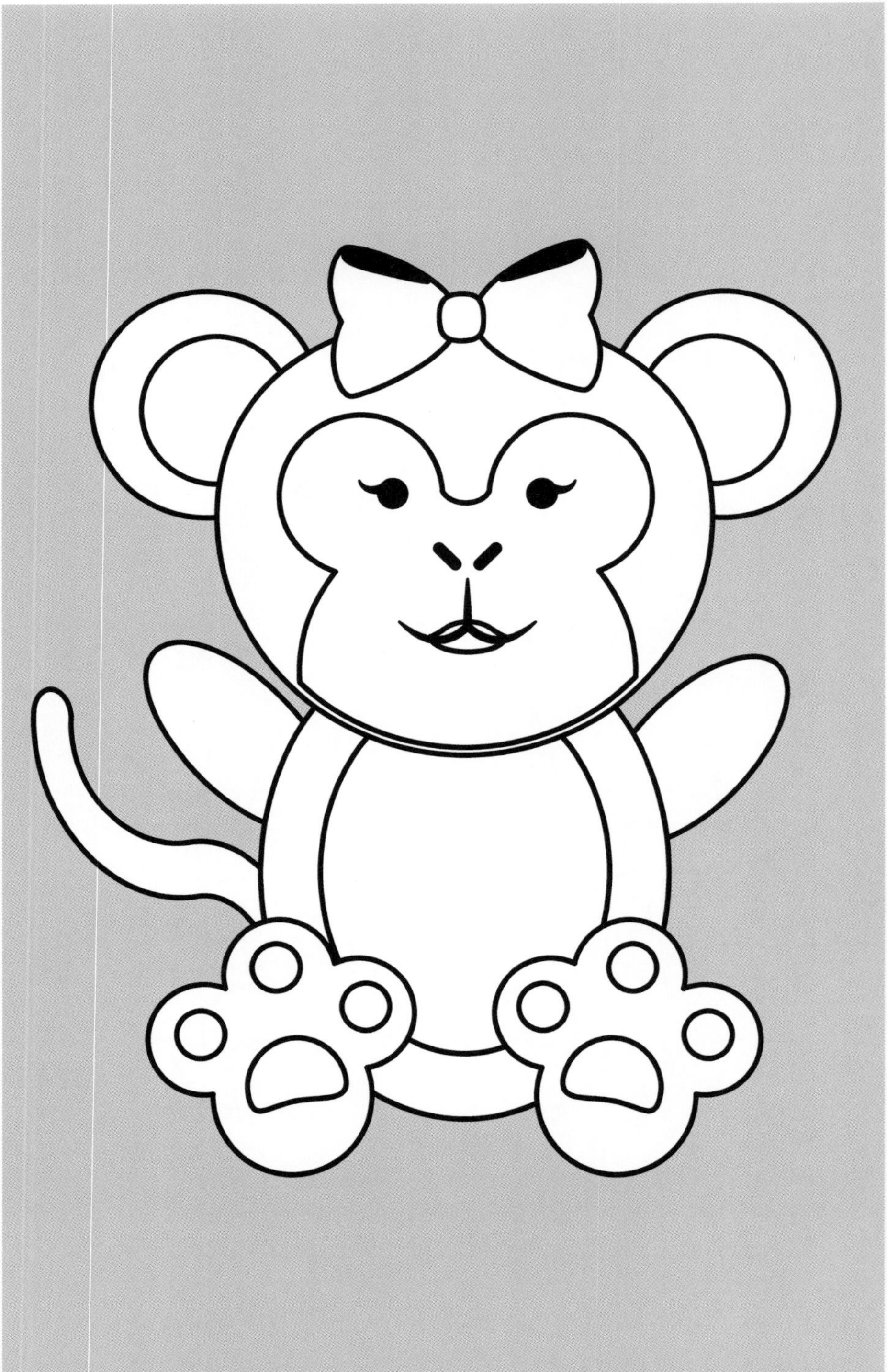

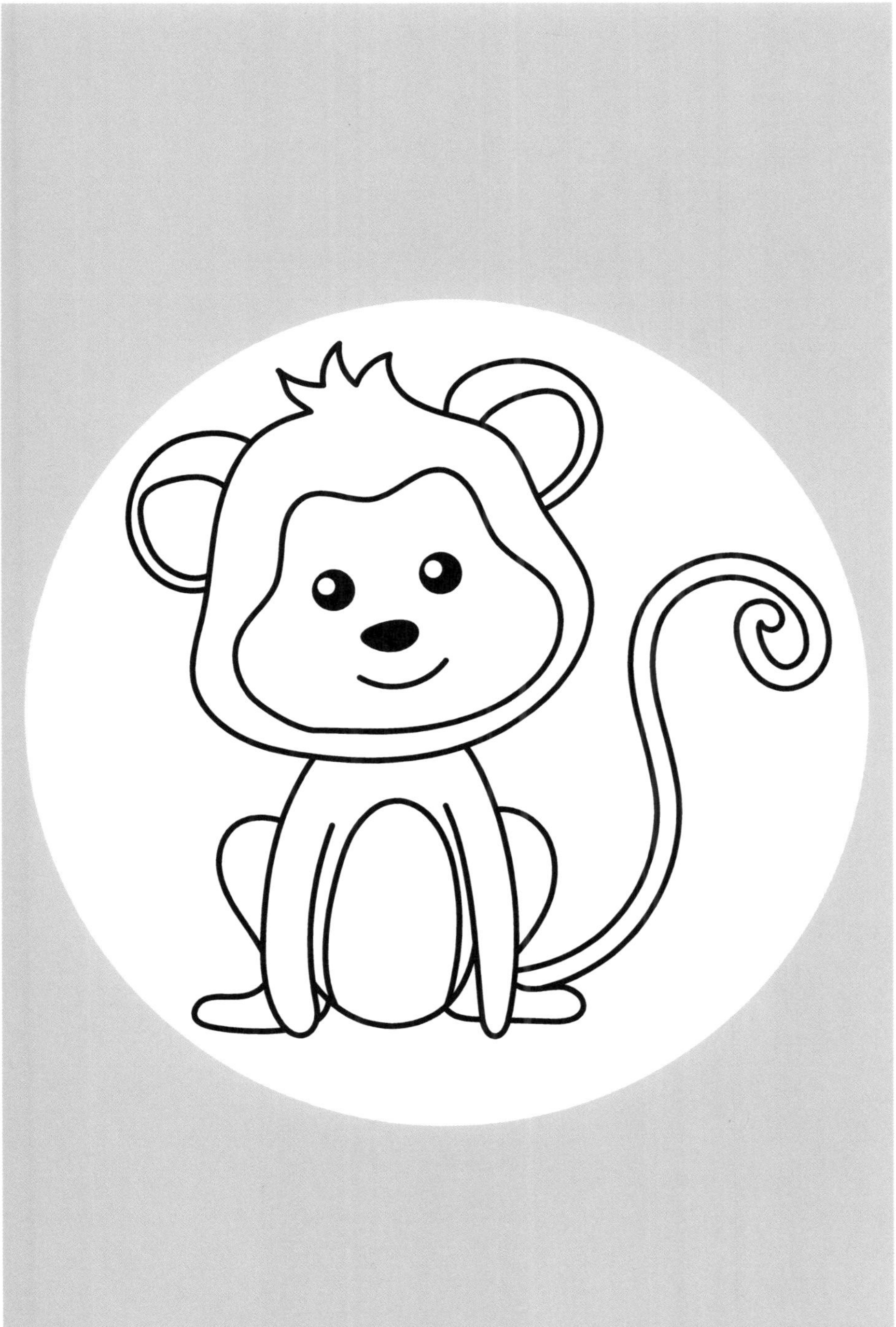

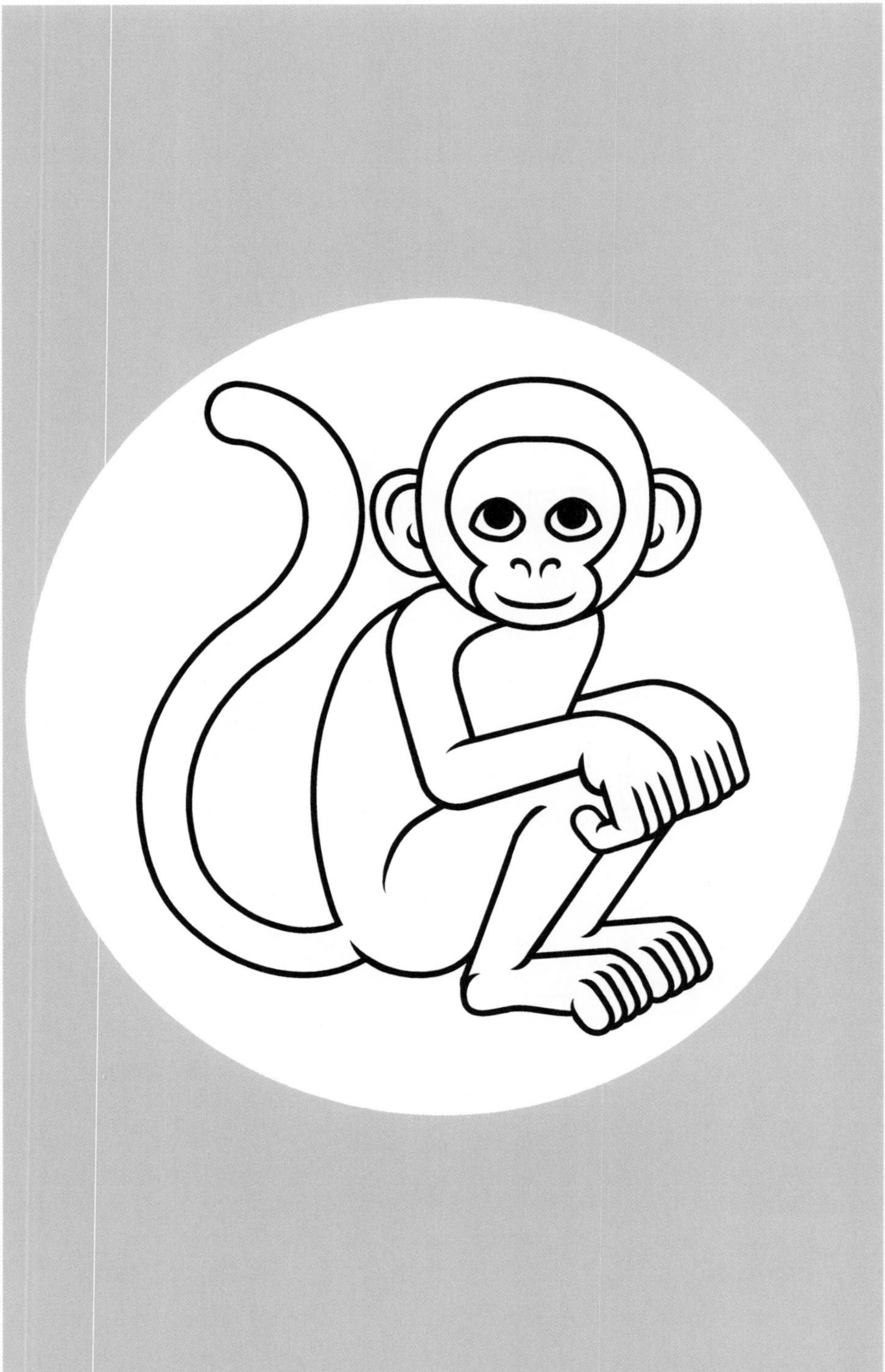

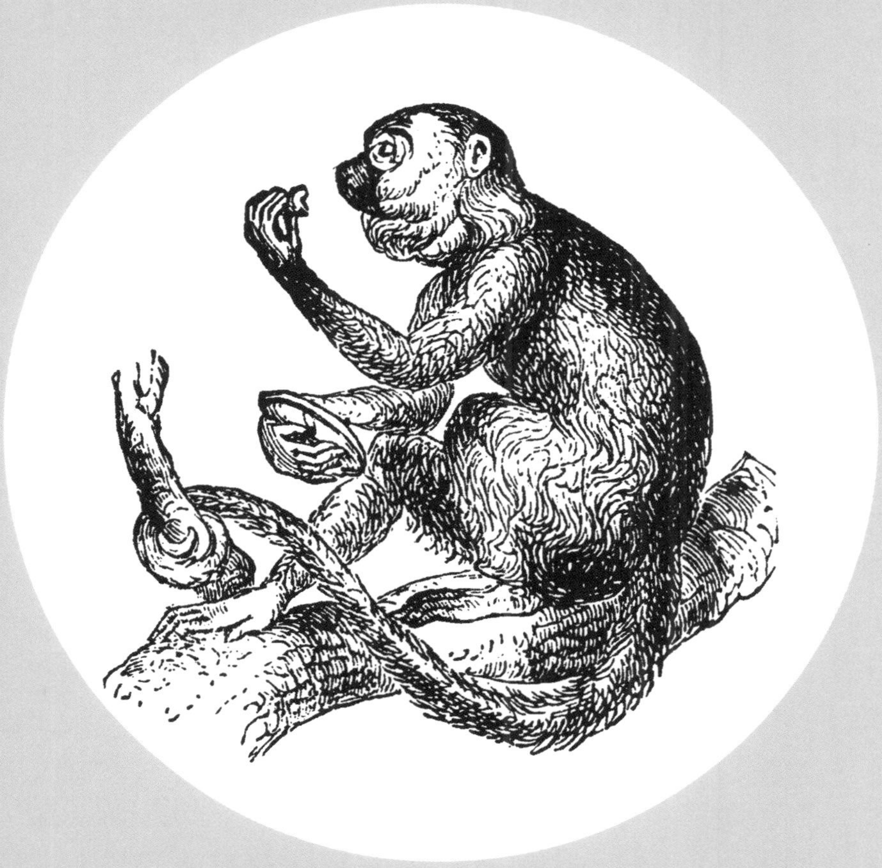

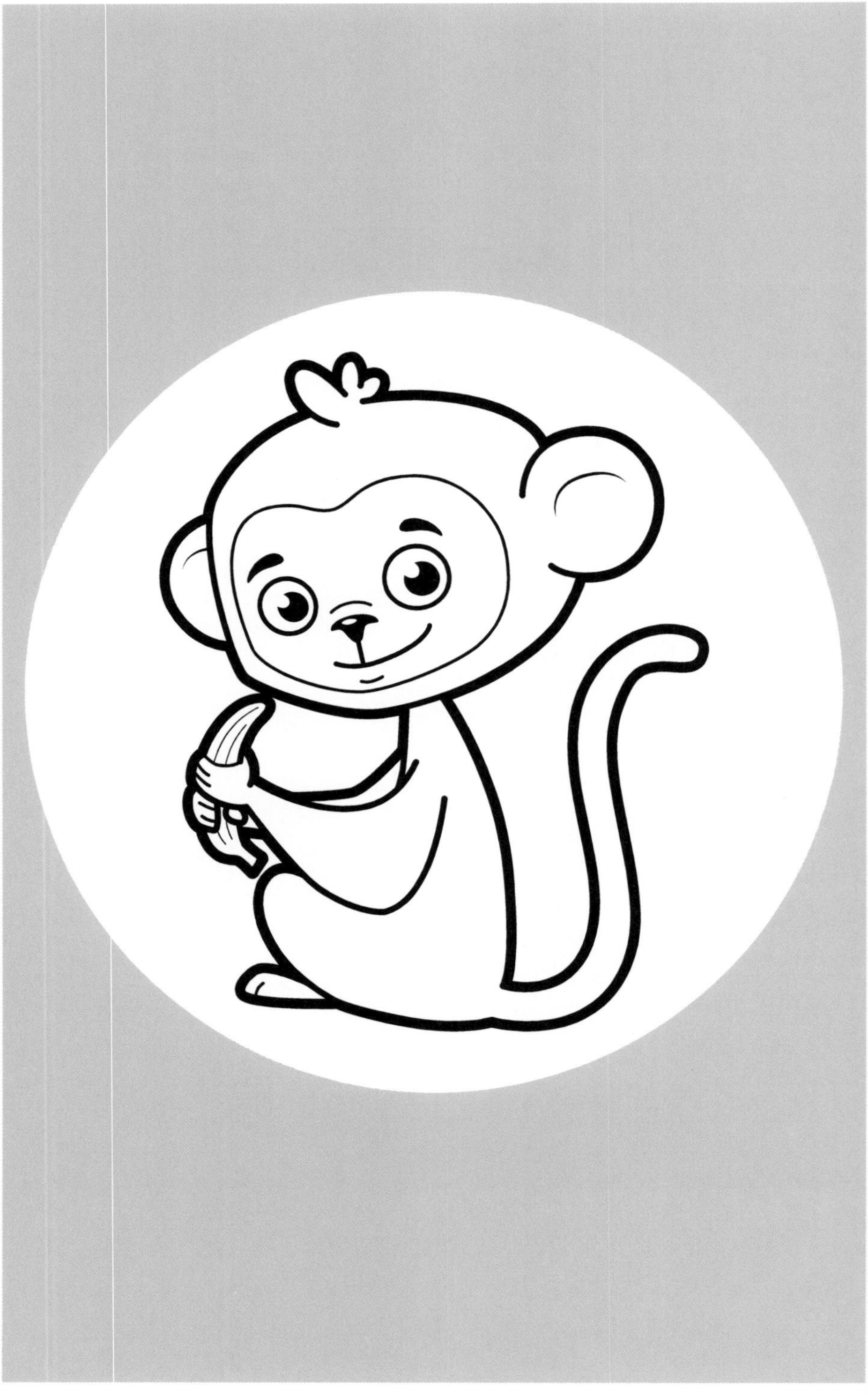

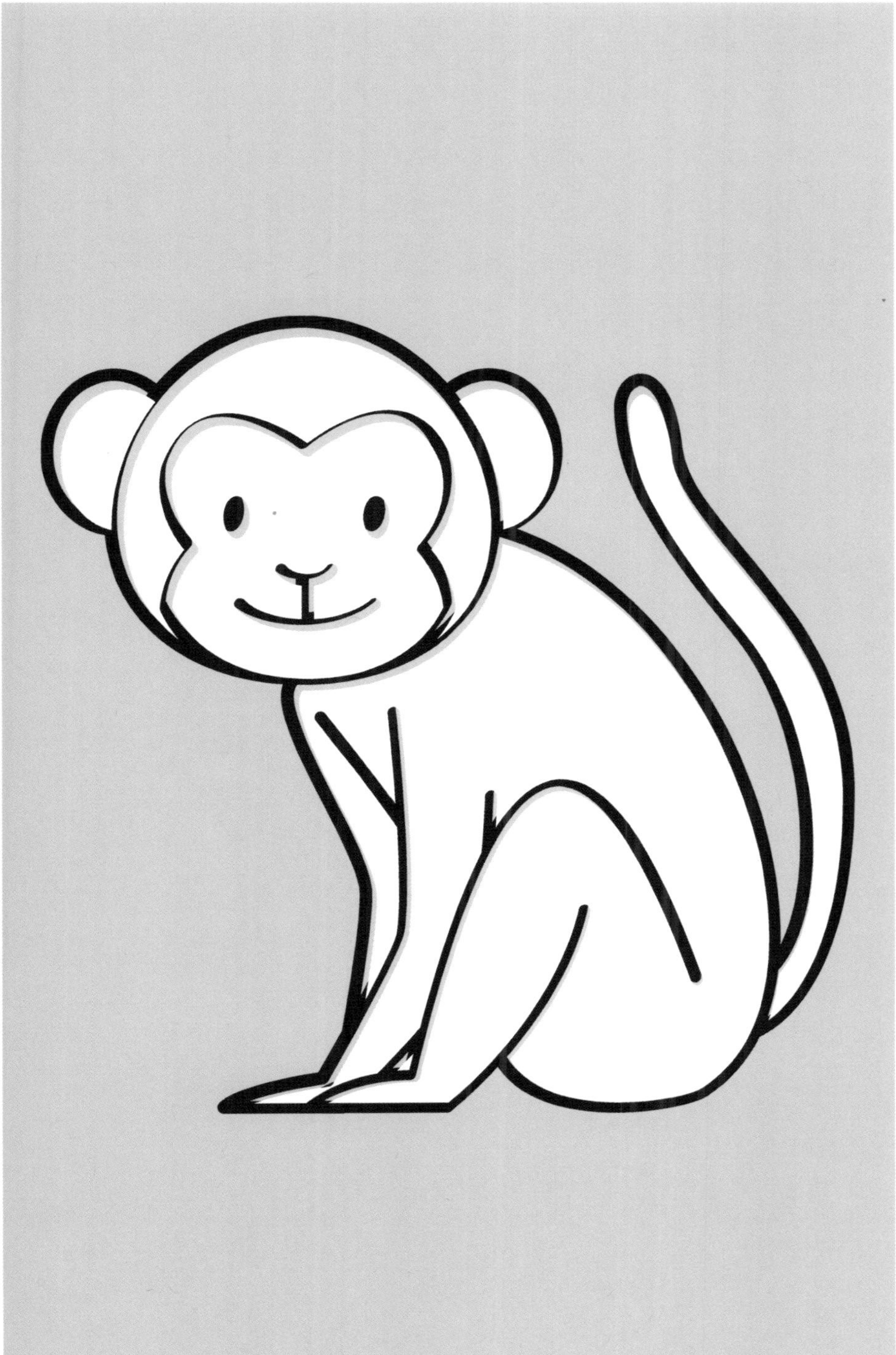

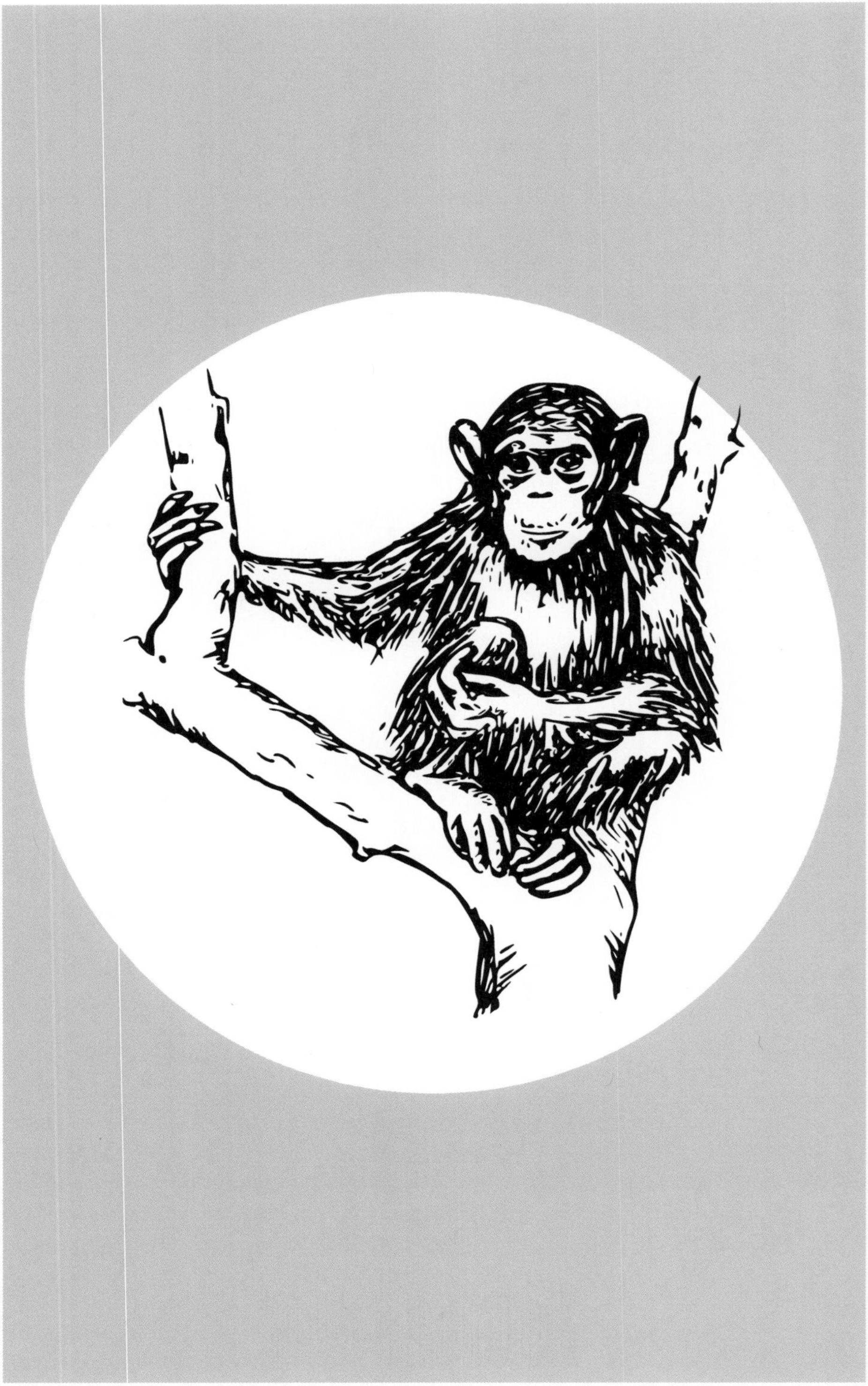

Printed in Great Britain
by Amazon

25024292R00018